The Clearing

Also by Louise Morgan Runyon:

Reborn (2004)

LANDSCAPE / Fear & Love (2007)

The Clearing

Poems

Louise Morgan Runyon

The Clearing

ISBN: 978-1-61005-099-9

This book is dedicated to my mother,
Marie Morgan Runyon

Contents

8   The Clearing

1.

12   the difference
14   table
15   dance church
17   holding the dance
18   Medlock School Powwow, 1988
19   Circles and Rows
20   Circle Game: Farmer in the Dell
21   so what kind of flowers
     bloom in the clearing?
22   The Clearing Dream
23   Rose Colored
25   Maelstrom Pantoum
26   Infusion

2.

30   Another presence
32   The Ride Dream
34   Neutral
35   Arugula
36   Witness, Trouble, Terrain

3.

40   The Angry Baby Poem
41   brush fire
42   airport
43   good girl
44   this girl
45   separate
46   color blind
47   The Red Candle
49   dear families

50   In the Southern Tradition

4.

54   time passage
55   sticks
56   compost kiss
57   teeth and earth
58   Beach dream
59   the swimmer
60   The Lumber Aisle at Home Depot
61   Prose Poem – The Clearing
62   Survive & Rescue
65   Survive & Rescue II
66   Bluebell Makes a Gratitude List

67   *Petunias in the Window*

78   *Acknowledgments*
79   *About the Author*

The Clearing

She had been told of a clearing,
and told that although she had been
in a dense forest for a long time,
she had come now
to a clearing space

She recognizes that the clearing
might in fact be large, immense;
she had imagined that the clearing, when spoken of,
was tiny, small and round – brief –
that it was surrounded by vast forest on all sides,
that it wouldn't take long at all to cross,
that it might contain a few stumps,
the charred remains
of a campfire –

She realizes that a clearing
may be the result of trees felled and cleared by man,
or occur naturally in a small state, in the middle of the woods
through forest fire, or flooding of the valley floor;
also that a clearing may be naturally occurring and vast –
as in grasslands, or prairie, or steppe –
where the deer go to graze at dusk,
what the hunters know

She knows that the dense forest supports
certain kinds of creatures, those that live in trees and others,
but that open land is required for vast birds to soar,
for herds and grazing mammals,
open land as is found in Africa and Siberia and Kansas,
for the gazelles and the antelope,
for the buffalo to roam

and that sometimes,
as the Cherokee explain in their myths,
there are otherwise unexplained vast open grasslands
that are whole mountains – the precious balds,

beloved of hikers

She understands that a clearing
may be a place to plant a garden,
to build a house, to start a farm,
and also that clear-cut
can be a tragic term

She is aware that the clearing she enters
may be enormous, and not without
its own exposing dangers,
but also with the room to herd, to bound, to grow, to fly,
perhaps, to group and gather,
to wave in the wind like the grasses themselves

and that this may be not only a path,
but a place for her
for a long upcoming time

1.

the difference

the last time I went to the temple, the priestess
joined my hand with my son's, and said
that I had come to a clearing,
that my path had taken me
through a dense forest for a long time,
but that I had come into a clearing,
and that sometimes the clearing
is the path

> *I had been to the Afro-Brazilian temple before.*
> *The first two times were painful.*
> *In the midst of all that open-throated, full-hearted,*
> *unthrottled singing and dance,*
> *I felt so isolated, my heart*
> *so constricted.*

last night as I lay in the cold dark
in my bed, I tried to figure out
what had made the difference in a year,
what had made the difference –
so that sometimes, times like today,
my heart billows out and my life is filled up
with unexpected people and unplanned endeavors
that quicken, enliven, enrich me

I searched and found
that within the last year I had found you,
and another new friend,
who have helped to make
such a difference

and no doubt it is me who has changed
so that this might happen,
but whenever it might have been that I had met you
in any of the years past,
I believe I would have stumbled upon the fact
that I needed to ask you to dance,

and that this would have made
such a difference

table

ten strangers sit cross-legged
in a circle on a wooden floor,
the floor a temporary table
suspended over earth

the strangers quiet, silent,
traffic from the Sunday morning world
sounding outside the window,
ten strangers make this still point,
choose to sit down, and then
to dance

two hours pass and the ten sit again –
the dance has reached its fever pitch,
children have peeked in through the door,
have been drawn in, the dance
has flowed and ebbed and flowed again

strangers have danced,
a train whistle has blown
deafeningly, outside the window;
the circle, the table, are again intact,
the train rumbles by
rhythmically, yet

dance church

what I know about my body
is the same thing I know
about my soul

– Bluebell

and so she must step up to the altar
of the internal music –
she must go, still, to dance church –
to the altar of her son and his friends,
the altar of the music that speaks aloud
to the quiet place inside her,
the place that is silent and stands still

and although going to this church
has brought her much pain in the past,
and even though she hasn't felt
she created something worthy,
though many may not have liked it or understood,
there is still a quiet place inside
that she must visit

and there have been times – many times –
and there will be times – how many times –
when what happens between herself and others
with whom she dances, herself especially,
but also that great and nameless audience which is out there,
that is a magic, a beating heart,
a flowing breath, a stopped moment
that is so important to all of us to know
and never to forget

and so, no matter the path,
however different or circuitous the route this time,
she must go, still, to dance church

and she must bring her son
and her son must bring her

and they must bring each other,
they must meet there

with all the other many
beating hearts

holding the dance

Bluebell says:

something sacred,
waiting to be held

the space is held by the circle of dancers,
as if for two kind wrestlers
in the ring

dancers
    who meet and roll,
        pause and wait,
            drop and fall,

                fly

Medlock School Powwow, 1988

on Earth Day the Native Americans came and reordered,
pushed back the straight lines of tables and chairs,
drew a huge circle of chalk on the floor,
ignored report cards and rulers, made the world round;
teachers and parents, principals and children
sat together on the floor in a circle –
the change, profound

inside the circle Jonathan Warrior did the hoop dance,
twenty hoops encircling his neck and his limbs –
he juggled and balanced them, stood on one foot,
he threw them and caught them, turned all around,
he jumped in the air, the children were rapt –
when one hoop began to fall, and then another –
the hoop dance fell apart, the hoops
lay on the ground

the MC for the day, William Eagle Hurt, said
that is how it is, children, sometimes
things fall apart

and he started to cry

there was surprise, a hush
as William remembered
his own falling apart,
the children, the alcohol, all that was lost

a grown man crying,
the children learned more on that round day
than on all the rectangular, triangular,
arrow-straight days
before

Circles and Rows

Circles of chairs versus chairs in rows,
clacking wooden folding chairs, in rows,
like graduation chairs on a huge lawn
(under white tents or blue sky),
the one man sitting in the last chair
on the last row, so far from front, distracted,
gazes out the open door
at the woman
walking by

Others of us sit on chairs in a circle,
the door closed, across the hall,
the circle a net into which
our tears and judgments fall

The warm circle,
where real people in real time
offer up real things,
the kind circle, the surroundings balm
to the long holiday weekend spent alone:
the in-chargeness of all that,
the having learned that one cannot ask
for too much

Circle Game: Farmer in the Dell

a figure in red, in the center –
crouched, crumpled,
red garment like the melted
wax of a candle

the static in her head loud,
she cannot hear the murmurs of the others,
her head dropped and vision blurred,
she cannot see

nevertheless, somehow in blindness
she steps backwards, away from center

at her back senses a little warmth
as she steps into the space behind her, finds
fingers, hands, that part from one another

her hands are taken
into the hands of others,
she becomes part of a circle
of cutout paper dolls
                        she is the red doll

her head lifts, she sees
everyone who has been in the circle
around her, the whole time

there may be even other circles
in front of her, behind

so what kind of flowers
bloom in the clearing?

Many – populating the vast
wildflower meadows of Patagonia,
California, Alaska, Scotland

and after rains –
the blooming of cactus overnight
in the desert

unique to the heath balds
of North Carolina at Roan Mountain,
the Gray's Lily, named for the botanist Asa Gray –
rare and red, bell-shaped, speckled

and there is the Texas bluebell,
member of the gentian family,
proliferating in the prairie, steppe and grasslands
of the American great plains

and then, the English bluebell –
lavender-blue and pendulous,
tubular with petals curled at the end,
pleasantly but strongly scented,
flowering and leafing early,
before the canopy closes

Among the stands of bare trees in England
the earth is purple, a carpet
of lavender-blue

> *...washing the brows and slacks*
> *of the ground with vein-blue...*
> *the bluebells in your hand baffle you...*[1]

---

[1] The italicized lines are by Gerard Manley Hopkins, from a journal
entry dated May 9, 1871.

The Clearing Dream

Sick in bed, freezing rain outside the window,
an image comes to her of scrounging
in a dark and rainy clearing –
a line drawing

thin, crackling lines
partially obscured by mist,
her own bony fingers enter her field of vision,
gather brush into teepees
all over the clearing –
later, to burn

teepees of black and inky lines, gathered at top,
sticking up from earth
like so many upside-down pigtails
of scraggling black hair

the gathered brush a promise
of clearing the field on the next clear day,
smoke giving way to blue sky and fresh growth
when the weather turns and the brush can burn,
now just icy bleakness, black and whiteness

when into the foreground of her vision come images
in full lush color of multiple, multi-colored quilts,
oranges and rose, yellows and reds,
purples and greens and black

and candles, two-tone roses, paintings,
a blue stuffed elephant

and sleep

Rose Colored

the birth of a baby, what about it
brings new tears, each time

perhaps it's the carrying on
of the tortured family line,
perhaps the promise of grandchildren
though this child is not one

is it simply birth,
the pushing through against odds,
green shoots through dark soil,
layers of dead matter

> *this baby's face full*
> *its tiny cap, fitted*
> *its clear brow, rosebud mouth*
> *its tiny hands, fisted*

> *its mother and father*
> *unmarried, beaming*

whatever –
a drive with wild abandon to the quilt store,
a finding of the softest, brightest flannels

and though this baby is a boy, his quilt
will be of the warmest rose
mixed with periwinkle, lemon,
pink polka-dotted orange, and lime

distinct from the other quilt-in-progress,
that one's deep blues and swirling yellows
reflecting the ocean-love and wild hair
of one who might someday
give grandchildren

this one will be quilted by hand, in hearts,
so unlike the flat, machine-stitched quilts
now in vogue, this one
will be thick
and full

Maelstrom Pantoum[2]

The arrival of the prodigal son, in snow
orange peel and melted chocolate on the stove
the tow truck pulls the car behind with dog inside
red curls spill and freckles glow

orange peel and melted chocolate on the stove
outrageous white fat flakes of maelstrom snow
red curls spill and freckles glow
the dog from the west is amazed at snow

outrageous white fat flakes of maelstrom snow
the pond fills, boots soak through, the water flows
the dog from the west is amazed at snow
we sit by the fire, eat chocolate-covered orange peel

the pond fills, boots soak through, the water flows –
next day the wood ducks reappear
we sit by the fire, eat chocolate-covered orange peel
the spring peepers gloat, we're here, we're here!

---

[2] The *pantoum*, a form developed by French poets in the 19th century, is derived from a 15th century Malayan folk poem. My poem does not follow the form strictly, but is an "imperfect *pantoum*."

Infusion

1.

        pushing against the edge
of sleep: an off-white art-paper box
    – rice paper or cotton rag –
four cubes making one, only one square surface seen,
across the four a charcoal drawing, a dust –
of mountains, a horizon, sky

towards the beginning of my waking,
crowding me out of my sleep,
some soft ink begins at center,
seeps, infuses the mountains with green

2.

long ago at Penland,
deep in the Blue Ridge Mountains,
outdoors and free-standing, the Craftsman's Shrine –
an upside-down *U*, flat at the top,
built with squared corners of native rock –
and my Great-Uncle Rufus with snow-white hair,
standing like an arrow in long white robes,
head towards heaven, arms spread low,
palms facing out in an upside-down *V*

I lift mine eyes up unto the hills, he said,
from whence cometh my help
from whence cometh my strength
from whence cometh balm
I lift mine eyes up unto the hills
he said at sunset, and we did

3.

my first-born son was born
on the same birthday as Uncle Rufus

what color was Uncle Rufus's hair
he asked, as an adult
what color was Uncle Rufus's hair
his own so red, now reddish-brown,
and so we had to ask

why, white – everyone said
white – even those
who had known him young –
but someone thought, just maybe,
that one time
it had been red

2.

Another presence

There is another presence in the clearing, tall and pale,
hair with glints of red, pale gold, and white,
eyes blue and green with hints of reddish brown,
there is another presence here –
we lie tangled in the long grass of the clearing,
drag our fingers through the other's hair

there is another presence here, tall and pale,
his voice is high and thin, it catches
in the clearing

our fingers have yet
to slip unseen through skin,
to pass through skin and bone to move inside
the other's chest and breath

our fingers yet to tweak, massage
the found open heart,
clear blockages, open channels,
moving softly, with precision

there is another presence in the clearing,
we ride horses and we swim the river;
he glides smoothly past me underwater,
passes me now swiftly on the trail,
then comes back around

we lie tangled once again
in the long, deep grass of the clearing,
our fingers fully deep now, inside the other's chest

no longer thin, his voice becomes
deep and rich, full and loud –
full, like the river,
loud, like the river

like the river
like the river
in which we swam

The Ride Dream

They both wore many things, he draped
in layers of wool and cotton, blankets and batting –
gray and olive and white; she fitted
in multiple coats and quilts,
all magnificent but
weighing down

> *they regard each other for a moment,*
> *then, with little provocation, she leaps*
> *onto his back, and they are away*

he gallops, immediately, she rides
barefoot and bareback, standing,
knees bent, arms aloft, hair flying,
quilts of silk held overhead,
color streaming out
behind

he executes a neat trick –
jumps into the air, clicks
all four heels together, lands;
she does a soft shoe, nonchalantly,
on his back

and so
they race and ride
across the desert, the field, the plain,
the ride answering many prayers

when suddenly, without warning,
he stumbles, fumbles;
front knees buckling, he slows to a limp,
goes down

the woman is thrown, attempts triage,
the horse rolls
off of his knees, onto his side,

does not respond

the woman, unbelieving, crazed,
drags sharp fingernails through crazy-colored quilts,
divides them into thin strips, plaits them, whips the horse,
threads and colors flying
overhead

the horse regards her
with one blindered eye

the woman wanders off, broils in the sun,
sheds coats and quilts, leaves a trail
of velvet and calico, corduroy and silk

the horse heaves and sweats, broils also,
rolls finally, piecemeal, onto his back,
shakes off the gray wool, the olive,
the heavy cotton batting;
still, the blinders stay

at night both are cold and naked,
he shivering in place, she wandering, lost;
she burying herself in sand
just before dawn

dawn mist lifts, revealing the two
are not so far apart –
both naked, both no longer
weighted down

miraculously, the horse,
able to bring his feet under him, stands

> *will the wind blow the hair from the woman's eyes*
> *will the horse man turn his blindered head*
> *will they look the other's way?*

Neutral

instead of a boxed animal,
a creature crowded into one interior wall
of a cardboard cage

rather than a flying cat, claws splayed,
eyes blazing, tongue spitting

instead of a weary human, hoeing in a field,
heart so heavily weighing down chest
it seems she hoes through mud

instead of these, a naked woman
walks silently up to a man,
quietly removes his jacket, belt,
carefully unties shoes, takes off socks,
helps him out of shirt and pants,
stands

nakedly in front of him, lightly touching,
breasts brushing chest, skin touching skin,
hands dangling next to hands

a woman, who extends her left arm
to place her left hand at the man's back,
who reaches her right arm to curve a palm
around the back of the man's head,
who lifts her lips to quietly, gently kiss the man

a woman
holding a man softly,
in neutral

Arugula

my twenty-something, generation-now children
laugh when I pronounce *uh-RUG-you-la,*
but it was only iceberg lettuce
we were served in the 50s

in any case I grow it now,
though still I struggle to pronounce,
and have eaten it a lot with you this fall, lately,
learning from restaurants that its sharpness is delicious
with dried fruits and sugared nuts,
to my own I add
marigolds

you brought me some, a gift
from Athens, Georgia, its organic market,
along with a smallish watermelon
which you tossed and punted
like a football in my yard

I eat *uh-RUG-you-la* now alone,
pick it in the freezing cold,
recall

Witness, Trouble, Terrain

She takes in the blue sharkskin shirt,
its tails hanging out
on this tornado night in Georgia,
the shirt the impossible color
of deep blue sex

she watches the popping of his gum,
each smack pushing her aside,
every crack keeping him
in his separate space;
in public, she is distanced

she hears his considered
choice of words,
words he would not, ordinarily, use

she feels his slight discomfort
and certain defiance –
it is not now a choice for him,
except between life and death

she senses the slim self-consciousness
of the new, tight pants,
the complete certainty that he must wear them
and that he wears them well

she notes the tilting
of his head back, non-habitual,
the cracking of his gum as he scans the stormy trees,
the black clouds of Georgia

cocksure, yet still uncertain,
an arrogance not previously tried on,
determined to try out bad, still hoping for the moral edge;
he knows that she knows this all,
and that every aspect of this display
keeps her away

what she knows is that he has come to a trailhead
and that he must take the lower path
as well as the higher one
just as certainly as he must grow older
every day

3.

The Angry Baby Poem

The angry baby says no,
it is not all right
for the father and the grandmother to fight,
for the father to leave
when the grandmother arrives,
for the feud to stop
its mother's milk

The angry baby says no, it is not OK
to sleep in a crib in a closet,
to be locked in a closet by a babysitter,
to have knife-wielding strangers in the home

The angry baby says no,
it will not give up its mother,
no matter how angry,
will not stop searching for its father,
no matter how long gone

brush fire

1.

Bluebell runs across the center of the field,
blazing torch in hand,
she stops, sets fire to brush,
runs, and stops again

around the perimeter now she streaks,
stops, lights more fires

Bluebell climbs a ladder
on one side of the clearing, yells across
do not come – you are not welcome –
do not come!

the fires catch,
small ones join other small ones,
the clearing erupts,
Bluebell watches chastened, but unafraid

the crackle and the heat lessen,
the blaze burns lower till it simply glows,
a great red sea burning in darkness,
then all is black

2.

it rains, time passes;
Bluebell stands at the edge of the clearing
surveying the charred field

she enters, walks through,
sinks to her knees at the sight
of tiny, tender shoots
pushing up green through blackened earth,
places her chest down,
breathes

airport

she steps into the airport as if into a former life, confused –
forgetting the need to tap the card
upon leaving the train station,
unable to remember if she must take
the boarding pass to the desk

she does not think about the quart-size ziploc bag,
which they seem no longer to enforce,
or the need to show her ID twice,
as required in her former life

she takes the rolling sidewalks, which she loves –
some are rolling, some are not today –
the fluorescence and the little pink lights
highlight the blue in stone and sky in the African display
as she rolls her new self on to Concourse A –
there are photos, rose and pink, of the nebulae
as she rolls on to Concourse C, all the way

a former self from a former life;
her new self sat out late last night,
inhaled the last fragrant gardenia
and the first pink sky,
her new self full and peaceful,
soft as the twilight night

her new self taking, just one moment at a time,
the heaving of the heavy carry-on,
the failure to remember the cushion for her back,
the never-failing rush of New York harbor air

good girl

a woman in a long, elegant,
dark plum coat with velvet collar,
a stylish figure, turns –

and in profile reveals
a large, protruding backpack, black,
a slim bouquet of unopened daffodils
from Georgia, sticking out
of its outside pocket

in profile, the woman trundles dutifully,
the good girl, dutiful daughter to
the good mother, now ninety-five

the woman turns once more
and is almost elegant, and stylish, again –

re-turns to profile, becomes
the school girl,
plodding methodically back home
from Georgia, backpack in tow

this girl

this is the girl
whose daddy left without a word,
and later left the world for good,
before she was grown enough
to find him

this is the girl who still
wore pigtails and freckles,
looked out at the school photographer,
smiled, and was brave

separate

two separate women
in long dresses, drawn waists,
hair piled high on heads,
two separate women of different ages,
equal adults: that possibility

two cameos in silhouette,
only one is taller, otherwise so close
as to be difficult to distinguish
any difference

two separate adults, that concept:
not bound, no pulls, no rage

similar –

yes, yes, yes, similar,
similar, but separate,
similar, but not the same

color blind

my mother, at 94, called in for a film shoot –
no red, no white, they said, and loved her
despite her blindness and her deafness,
despite her broken hip-ness,
her over-expressiveness –
show no emotion at all
the director said

gave her a dress
of red, black, white
and green with yellow diamonds,
let her wear it
home

my own trademark colors
of red, black, white:
the cleanness,
the purity
of them

The Red Candle

1.

I light the red candle at noon,
the moment my mother is scheduled
to go before the knife –
she gave me life, she gave me life,
the most and the least
that can be said

2.

she found a home for us when I was four,
when I asked her,
where is our home, mommy
where is our home

for two years after my father left we shuttled
between 115th Street and Morningside Drive,
between Penland, North Carolina and Reno, Nevada,
dropping beloved and bedraggled Floppy
somewhere along the way

we lived with Mrs. Schmidt, who was old,
and the Joneses, who were young,
and their three small boys
who were wild, and scared me,
my crib in a closet
behind French doors

that is why, she says,
she fought so hard to keep the apartment,
to save the building,
why she took on the New York megaliths and monoliths,
why she wouldn't give up,
why she made a career of it,
finally winning

but I think perhaps
there is another reason,
her own childhood spent shuttling
from one rented house to another
in the mountains of North Carolina,
no more than two years in any one town,
my mother never mentions
this

3.

I am letting the red candle burn,
its wax streaming and pooling like a red bridal train,
the red candle in its pewter holder
made by my cousin,
pewter of the same dogwood design
shaped and pounded by our self-same grandfather,
three-quarters of a century ago
at Penland

I am letting the red candle burn
while my mother goes under
the knife

dear families

the young, black, homeless mother, an orphan from Florida – no family, no backup – gets work in a nursing home in Webster, North Carolina on an unseasonably hot weekend in May

she packs her 8-year old son into the car they call home, along with cold drinks and snacks, crayons and paper, checks on him every hour as she changes the diapers, transfers from wheelchair to bed the old, white people in the nursing home

they ask if she can work longer, a double, an extra shift, she needs the money, hesitates, says yes, keeps checking on her son

the letter to the families of nursing home residents is unexplained and shocking: *dear families, there has been a murder, a body found in the parking lot* – what on earth, I ask my cousins, it wasn't like that, they say

the woman goes out to her car one last time, in the heat of the day, and although she has kept the windows partly open, the boy, as if sleeping, is dead

she panics, tries CPR, tells someone, wraps him in a blanket, drives away; is arrested in Asheville, vilified in the Sylva paper, is charged with second degree murder, sits for a year in the Sylva jail

some citizens object, visit her, raise money, place her on prayer lists, hire a lawyer

she is acquitted, found "not guilty" in a packed courtroom, a rare act of justice; "it is rare for justice to be so great and so pure, and it is a beautiful thing," said her lawyer; Jackson County citizens help her find a job

she steps into her life again; for the first time, she visits her son's grave

In the Southern Tradition

the jig is up with Marie
my father told my part-sister,
and left a note on the pincushion
in the Southern tradition

did he even look back
at me, his two-year old,
asleep in my crib

he didn't come back, ever –
already I had spoken my first words:
bye-bye, daddy, gone

eleven years later he died,
a heart attack,
no chance for me to hunt him down,
no funeral, no grave,
his obituary saying he didn't want either,
but the newspaper said
I was his daughter

forty-six years later, seven of us
gather around a woodstove
on a late December afternoon

I place the fifty-eight-year-old valentine
inscribed from Pa to me,
along with a one-hundred-and-five-year-old
lock of golden hair, his

and pictures, from all the ages
of his grandchildren and me,
place them in a white box
tied up with red ribbon,
say all there is I have to say

everyone speaks

though no one knew him

we carry the small box out,
place it in a hole,
hold long-stemmed pink roses
in a circle around the grave,
throw them in

in the dusk, each of us shovels
dirt, the blue ceramic headstone,
cracked in the kiln in several places,
reads "Father"

we begin "Amazing Grace" in the Southern tradition
and hear a howl – as the never-demonstrative dog Solo
scrambles into our midst,
turns to face us with his other-worldly eyes,
through all the many verses of the song

night falls, we go back in,
eat sweet potatoes and ham,
good Southern food;
through the window we can see
outside, in the night, the candles
we left burning

4.

time passage

when the man that I love
has gray hair and a white beard

when what moves me the most about him
are the wrinkles
at the back of his neck

sticks

she is a tiny stick, this aged woman,
grasping her cane with twig-like fingers
to creep

how many more times
will she make this trip
downhill

compost kiss

a kiss as we turn the compost barrel –
your gray and white, grizzled face,
beard trimmed to reveal pink lips

four hands are needed
to bring the barrel over the top,
rich rot tumbling, next year's riches

your arms are those
of a brown, furry animal, small paws;
your jaw bone taut, your beard
at its corners darker, swirls of gray-black hair
in close concentric circles

your bright eyes those
of an inquisitive, curious, hopeful,
intelligent creature

teeth and earth

my teeth have been exported to Israel
via digital satellite image,
they will come back to me through New Jersey,
in the shape of a golden crown

my airplane reservations from Atlanta to San Francisco
have been exported to India,
along with AOL customer service –
who knew?

I have had conversations in fairly clear English
with Arnold, Antonette and Edgar;
when I ordered the shirt I asked the woman,
are you in India, too?
I believe she smiled over the wires as she said,
no, Indonesia

I am about to travel to Peru,
where I will stay in the home
of an indigenous Peruvian person
on a floating island made from reeds,
re-constructed once every thirty years
in Lake Titicaca

"where home is home and known is known,
and sometimes strangers come"

Beach dream

Reclining on a rickety, navy blue chaise,
Bluebell's eyes, half-open, take in
the bright blueness of the ocean,
the diamond whiteness of the sand,
a heron who has no fear –

its long outrageous wispy plumes
streaming behind its tiny head, the heron
waits for the fisherman
to toss it a fish

Bluebell's eyelids descend, close –
she breathes in heat and sun, expanse of time,
descends to the bottom of the sea, floats up

the windows of her eyelids open
just a crack, she spies
her own two skeletal feet
sticking up from the rickety chaise,
her windows open slightly wider, she sees
a gleam of bones, oyster-shell and pearly,
rising from the sand

she lifts her eyes in dream to travel up
to knobby, pearly knees, and there –
an unaccountably tall skeleton, smiling –
just like Big Bird, without the feathers

benign and kind and grateful to be free,
free from the closet in which she's kept him –
Bluebell doesn't know who he is, but

my freedom's yours and yours is mine, says he,
the beach can also be a clearing,
and the sea

the swimmer

the swimmer is afraid of water,
having experienced early on
a deep and treacherous
undertow

the swimmer grew up
in the city, and the mountains, in the 50s –
no swimming pools, no lakes in either place
and elders afraid of water too –
she did not learn
until a cousin on her father's side
taught her – and only on her back,
in a humongous pool
in an old, once-grand
hotel in Brooklyn, in May
of her high school senior year

in college the swimmer learned
side stroke, breast stroke, crawl
and has been swimming ever since,
though still has fear of water –
prefers pools with bottoms, edges, sides,
still she swims, hardly ever passing others,
but hardly ever stopping

the swimmer has dived only once,
and only in order to graduate
from college

born under the sign of Cancer,
the swimmer swims peacefully amid
the splashers and the crashers,
the flipper-wearers, the kids

she-crab intuitive, a water child –
despite her fear has need for immersion,
surround sound, being held

The Lumber Aisle at Home Depot

Wide and empty, I could almost stride there, like a man,
owning the place, that male world, as I did once
the vast open warehouses, the mile-long mills,
the uncluttered roads of Atlantic Steel

I almost forgot that in my steel-toed boots
I trod in confidence there, belonging –
marched through the empty spaces between stacked mill stands,
strode down the dark and empty steel-cindered roads,
wrote a poem

felt in the deserted warehouse
the sacredness of a stage crossing
in a dark and empty theatre

Prose Poem – The Clearing

circles and squares, compass points and bearings, circumferences and radii; new stages, new eras and new beginnings

skirting the clearing, reaching across the divide, dashing through mist, setting fire to brush; summits, powwows

airports, warehouses, vast open spaces; echoes and symmetries, concentricities; archetype, felicity, coming and going; becoming, coming around

forest, floodplain, fabric and quilts; wetlands, wildfire, deserts and sand; no-man's land

circle of the hearth, homes and homelessness; square dance, circle dance, ring around the rosy; mythical, whimsical, the farmer in the dell

Survive & Rescue

Stage directions: *A dance*
for four women and one man,
with narration

Directions:
house lights go out, the stage is dark –
out of blackness, the strike of a match
illuminates a face, stage right;
the strike of another match
illuminates another face,
stage left

> **Narrator:**
> *earthquake, typhoon, tsunami*

Directions:
two candles are lit, one right and one left,
two figures are seen, one left and one right,
the man brings his candle, joins the woman on the right,
they crouch behind the candle flame;
their clothes are dense –
black, white, heavy

> **Narrator:**
> *Myanmar, Thailand, China, New Orleans*
> *Iraq, Philippines, home*

Directions:
within the darkness, upstage center,
another three figures appear –
tall and pale, thin, wearing white
translucent nightgowns

> **Narrator:**
> *one hundred thousand dead*
> *five million homeless*
> *one hundred fifty-five thousand drowned*

three thousand missing
two thousand gone
one, just one
alone

Directions:
the man and the woman in black and white
warm their hands over the flames of candles,
regard each other's face, find solace

Directions:
the group of three in their nightgowns float
to stand behind the woman and the man,
a white arm touches the sleeve
of a black jacket, from behind,
its wearer had never imagined
such warmth

Directions:
the three pale figures crouch down
behind the denser ones,
become illuminated now
in candle flame

Directions:
the man and the woman in black and white
feel networks, cobwebs, lace,
connections to the others

      Narrator:
      the disasters of
      1871, 1906, 1929
      2003, 2004, 2005
      2008, 2008, 2009

Directions:
the man and the woman fall back,
are caught, held, righted by the three,
a long white hand emerges from a pale gown
to touch the woman's dark face

Narrator:
the disasters of
Monday, Tuesday, Thursday
Saturday night, Sunday morning

Directions:
the weight of a pale hand from behind
comes to rest on the man's
black-jacketed chest,
the chest breathes

Narrator:
heartbreak, loneliness, devastation
survival

Directions:
the three tall figures drift off,
the two follow, come around, face them,
place their hands
on chests

Directions:
around a fire, center,
the pale ones and the dense ones hunker,
reach into pockets, find bits of bread,
offer them around

Directions:
lights come up to softly suffuse
the stage with yellow,
then fade to black
on count of ten

Survive & Rescue II [3]

two figures, dense in their black and white clothes,
the weight of a hand comes to rest,
each finds solace in the face of the other

candles are lit, one face finds another,
breath finds life in a black-jacketed chest,
the white-clothed sister, the black-clad brother

three figures in darkness, a saint or a mother,
white translucent nightgowns over breasts;
present, in darkness, like an absent father

typhoon, tsunami, wreak havoc, make bother,
struck matches reveal the pale guests;
three figures in darkness, a saint or a mother

around a fire, the five figures hunker,
lean together, both the pale and the dense,
the guests reach in pockets, find bread, offer;
the two, in their black and white clothes, accept

---

[3] This poem is inspired by the *villanelle* form, which entered English-language poetry in the 19th century based on the form of a French country song. My poem does not follow the form strictly.

Bluebell Makes a Gratitude List

Bluebell's got sisters, and she's got brothers
She's got a father, and she's got mothers
Bluebell's got a tricycle, and she's got a horse
She's got the strokes, and she gets the jokes

Bluebell has flowers, and she's got the farm
She's got vegetables, and she's got fruit
She's got bluebirds, and she's got jays
She's got the woodpeckers and the cardinals, all ways
Bluebell's got the birdhouse, and she's got the yard
She does what she does, sometimes it's hard

Bluebell's got chipmunks, and she's got squirrels
She's got baby rabbits, and baby girls
She's got red roses, and she's got yella
She's got a gal, and she's got a fella
Bluebell's whimsical, take it or leave it
She's got what it takes, you'd better believe it

     Bluebell has moves –
She's got a ballgown, and she's got jeans
She's got the ways, and she's got the means
Bluebell's got the sunset, and she's got the dance
Bluebell has everything, Bluebell takes a chance

Bluebell leads searches, and she performs rescues
She performs poetry in all kinds of venues
Bluebell's got youth, and she's got wisdom
The girl's got a path, and she's got a vision

Bluebell's got colors, and she's got words
Bluebell gets seconds, and comes back for thirds

Petunias in the Window

A story for children and adults

Drawings by Suzanne Clements

PETUNIAS
IN THE WINDOW

A story for grandchildren, as yet unborn

Shhhhh, I am going to tell you a story, child…

Yes, it is true.

And yes, it has a happy ending… and it doesn't have an ending… and it does…

Once upon a time, a little girl grew up in New York City, way up at the top of a big building, all the way up on the sixth floor. The little girl's name was Bluet.

Bluet lived in an apartment building, where sometimes people live as high as 60 floors!

People live in all kinds of places. In fact the little girl Bluet, who is now all grown up, has a granddaughter named Violet, and Violet lives in a YURT.

What is a YURT? It's a kind of a house from Mongolia, with round walls and a round roof with a point on top, like a very fat upside-down ice cream cone. And Violet, the granddaughter of Bluet, lives in a yurt, only her yurt is in the gold and rolling hills of California, and Violet has wild and swirling red and golden hair, just like her daddy…

But the little girl Bluet, who is now a grandmother, whose granddaughter Violet lives in a yurt, a long time ago lived at the very top of a building in New York City, all the way up on the sixth floor.

And this building was
filled with lots of people,
who all lived in small sections
of it called apartments,
sort of like compartments.
At night the building
would be all lit up,
filled with people
eating and
doing
homework and cooking
and playing. And at Christmas
you could see Christmas trees
in lots of the windows,
all lit up too.

Then one day the owner of the building, who was called the
Landlord, put up a sign in the lobby telling everyone to MOVE!

The sign told all the families and the old people and the little
children and the mothers and the fathers to find another place to
live. To move, to get out, to VACATE the building.

Lots of people did move. They were scared, and the Landlord
gave some of them some money, and they left.

But some stayed.

And the mother of Bluet, the little girl who is a grandmother now, was one of the ones who stayed. The mother of Bluet was named Petunia.

And not only did Petunia stay, but she fought the Landlord.

She organized other people to fight the Landlord. They told the Landlord they weren't going to move, they were going to stay in their apartment homes.

The Landlord said *NO.* He said *YOU HAVE TO GO.*

But they didn't, not all of them. Some stayed. And not only did they stay but they marched, and wrote letters, and one time they set up all their rocking chairs across the avenue and rocked in them and stopped traffic. And the Landlord couldn't help it, he couldn't make everyone move.

But there were other buildings – five other buildings – that the Landlord wanted to tear down. And one by one, people moved out of those buildings. And one by one, those buildings were torn down.

There were five families, though, who wouldn't leave the little girl's building. And so this building stayed standing – it did not get torn down.

But the building was dark now at night, except for just a few lights burning. The Landlord didn't take care of it anymore and lots of times it was cold there, and it leaked when it rained – really, really badly.

There was only one good thing. After the other buildings were torn down, Bluet could see from her mother's kitchen window a tiny angel, blowing its horn on the tip-top of the church way up the street from her apartment building. Bluet used to look at this angel from her mother's kitchen window.

Then Bluet grew up,
and moved away.

But her mother stayed and the
few other people stayed, and they
kept on fighting. The Landlord lived
just six blocks away, and the people and
their friends would go up there and stand
outside and hold up signs, and one time they
went *inside* and refused to leave. And when their
building had no heat and no hot water and when the
elevator stopped working, the people refused to pay their rent.

And then the mother, Petunia, started planting petunias!

Do you know what petunias are like? They are soft flowers, a
little bit like soft dog's ears and kind of sticky, and they smell
very sweet and a little bit dusty. When you hold them up to your
nose and sniff them, your sniff pulls them up to your face and
they cover your nose and your mouth like a mask.

So Petunia, the mother of the little girl named Bluet, planted petunias in something called window boxes, because in New York City there are no yards. She put the window boxes out on her windowsills all the way up on the sixth floor. And she always planted red, white, and purple petunias.

Down below, the people walking by would look up past all the boarded-up windows all the way up to the sixth floor, and there at the top would be red, purple and white petunias!

At night the mother of the little
girl would burn all her
lights, and the lights
at night and the
petunias during
the day were like
a beacon to the
people below, saying,
"Someone's home!"
and "We live here!"
A beacon is a light
telling people
where it's safe,
and where to go.

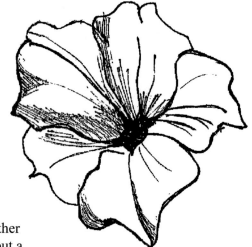

And sometimes the mother
of the little girl would put a
Christmas tree in her window, too.

And then, there came a day. There came
a day when the Landlord gave up.

One day, finally – after 41 years! – he gave up. The Landlord was tired and he realized he couldn't win, he couldn't fight the families who had stayed anymore. So he decided to fix up the building and let more people, new people, live there. And he decided to give the building a name – and he named it after the little girl's mother.

He put up a sign, and the sign said:

```
PETUNIA'S  BUILDING
```

And he put up another sign, and that sign read:

```
PETUNIA FOUGHT, AND
SHE WOULDN'T MOVE,
AND SHE ORGANIZED
OTHERS, AND SHE
PLANTED PETUNIAS, AND
SHE BURNED LIGHTS,
AS A BEACON.
```

Petunia is very old now, and she is nearly blind and can't see very well. But she still lives in the building and lots of people come to see her, and help her, and learn from her.

The little girl Bluet, who is now all grown up, comes too. She is very happy that now her mother lives in a building that isn't dark, and doesn't leak, and isn't cold.

The little girl's mother,
Petunia, doesn't plant petunias
anymore – the Landlord built a tall building right next door
and blocked out the sun. There isn't enough sunlight now for
petunias, and you can't see the little angel blowing its horn on
the top of the church up the street anymore.

This was the angel the little girl always used to look at from her
mother's kitchen window. It was like a beacon, too.

But the angel is still there, and when the little girl Bluet comes to
visit her mother, she stops on the street and looks up at the tiny
angel. It is still blowing its horn on the very tip-top of the church,
way up the street.

And sometimes Bluet, who is a grandmother now, goes to the
gold and rolling hills of California to visit her granddaughter,
Violet. Violet, who has wild and swirling red and golden hair,
just like her daddy, and lives in a –

YURT!

Petunias In The Window – Post Note

In 1954 Louise and Marie Runyon moved into 130 Morningside Drive on Manhattan's upper west side; Louise was 4 years old. In 1960 Columbia University, owner of the building, attempted to evict its tenants and those of five adjacent buildings, in order to build a new College of Pharmacy. By 1965, 130 Morningside was the only building of the original six left standing, and only five of its original 24 units remained occupied. The university gutted the unoccupied apartments and boarded up their windows, and the building remained that way for the next thirty-five years.

Columbia, seeking to improve its public image, decided in 2000 to renovate 130 Morningside Drive. The building was thoroughly re-done inside and out, and the five original tenants kept their apartments at rent-controlled prices. The remaining apartments were broken up into smaller units for graduate student housing, and the new Columbia School of Social Work was built next door. The building was named for Marie Runyon, and these two plaques now adorn the front of 130 Morningside Drive:

MARIE RUNYON COURT

and

This building is dedicated in
honor of Marie Runyon in recognition
of her more than
fifty years of service in the
Morningside Heights
and Harlem communities
as a member of the
New York State Assembly,
founder and Director of
the Harlem Restoration Project,
and tireless civil rights and
housing advocate.

Acknowledgments

My deepest appreciation goes to fellow-poets Michael Mack and Chelsea Rathburn, my two editors, for their inspiration, challenge, enthusiasm, rigor, and support. With them and with artist Suzanne Clements, this has become a collaborative project of fitting the pieces of the puzzle together, and a rich experience of learning and growth. My special thanks to Suzanne for her wonderful artwork, and to my son, Lucas Barth, for his beautiful photograph. I appreciate, also, others who read the manuscript and gave feedback – Adam Cole, Valerie Gilbert, Susanne Fincher and Marcia King – and early readers of *Petunias in the Window* including Sam, Hope and Jennie Williams, Tom Bell, Collin Kelley, Ann Ritter, Francis Goldin, and the little girl on the plane. I thank my son, Brian Barth, for translating the message about the clearing from Portugese into English for me, and Temple Guaracy in Santa Cruz, California for delivering that message. I am grateful to Memye Curtis Tucker and my fellow poets at Callanwolde Fine Arts Center for their feedback; to Several Dancers Core and The Field, where many of these poems first took breath; and to Judith Ortiz Cofer and fellow poets at the Southern Women Writers Conference for their critical response. My special thanks to Yvonne Bradford for her wisdom in graphic design, and to Emily Vorder Bruegge for her emergency computer help.

My deep appreciation also goes to those who contributed financially to the publication of this book: Janie Alexander, Joyce Allen, Paul Barth, Claudia Crenshaw, Clara Davis, Mary Elvington, Wendy Forbush, Michael de Give, Sarah Lopez, Maureen Nolan, Charlie Orrock and Teresa Paine, Deborah and Jay Palmer, Laurel and Perrin Radley, and Jim Skillman.

My thanks as well to all those anonymous friends in many different circles for furthering the concept of the clearing for me. Finally, my deepest thanks and appreciation to my mother, Marie Runyon, for her story and example.

About the Author

Louise Morgan Runyon holds a B.A. in English and Theatre Arts from Oberlin College, and is a modern dancer/choreographer as well as poet. She is Artistic Director of Louise Runyon Performance Company which has presented dance, poetry, puppetry and music at Atlanta venues since 1989. She has toured her one-woman show, *Crones, Dolls and Raging Beauties,* throughout the Southeast and the nation, and has performed her poetry in New Mexico, New York, Oregon, Kentucky and North Carolina, at the Southern Women Writers Conference in Rome, Georgia, and in Atlanta at venues including DeKalb County Public Library, Shambhala Center, Decatur Book Festival, the High Museum, Callanwolde Fine Arts Center, Emory University, 7 Stages, Decatur Arts Festival, Java Monkey Speaks, Barnes & Noble, Charis Books, Very Special Arts Georgia Gallery, Portfolio Center and the Arts Festival of Atlanta. She published her first book of poems, *Reborn,* in 2004 and her second, *LANDSCAPE / Fear & Love,* in 2007. Her work has appeared in *Java Monkey Speaks, Volumes I, II* and *IV,* and in *Golden Poetry: A Celebration of Southern Poets 50 and Older, Volumes II* and *IV;* "The Clearing" first appeared in Volume IV. Runyon is a practitioner of the FELDENKRAIS METHOD® of somatic education, a movement-based mind-body discipline. www.FeldenkraisAtlanta.com, www.LouiseRunyonPerformance.com.

79

Front Cover Photo: Lucas Barth
www.LucasBarth.com
Back Cover Photo: Michael de Give
Drawings and Back Cover Art: Suzanne Clements
www.sclements.com
Graphic Design: Yvonne Bradford

To contact Louise Morgan Runyon
about poetry performances:

Louise Morgan Runyon
P.O. Box 33601
Decatur, Georgia 30033-0601
LouiseRunyon@aol.com

To order this book, or for information
about upcoming performances:

www.LouiseRunyonPerformance.com